# A Pet's Life

# Goldfish

## Anita Ganeri

Heinemann Library
Chicago, Illinois

**www.heinemannraintree.com**
Visit our website to find out more information about Heinemann-Raintree books.

**To order:**
☎ Phone 888-454-2279
▣ Visit www.heinemannraintree.com to browse our catalog and order online.

© 2009 Heinemann Library
an imprint of Capstone Global Library, LLC
Chicago, Illinois

Customer Service: 888-454-2279

Visit our website at www.heinemannraintree.com

Printed and bound by South China Printing Company Ltd

13 12 11 10 09
10 9 8 7 6 5 4 3 2

**Library of Congress Cataloging-in-Publication Data**
New edition ISBN: 978 14329 3391 3 (hardcover) – 978 14329 3398 2 (paperback)
The Library of Congress has cataloged the first edition as follows:
Ganeri, Anita, 1961-
  Goldfish / Anita Ganeri.
    v. cm. -- (A pet's life) (Heinemann first library)
Includes bibliographical references (p.    ).
Contents: What is a goldfish? -- Goldfish babies -- Your pet goldfish --
Choosing your goldfish -- Setting up your tank -- Putting in plants -- Welcome home -- Feeding time -- Cleaning the tank -- Growing up -- A
healthy goldfish -- Old age.
  ISBN 1-4034-3998-2 (hardcover) -- ISBN 1-4034-4271-1 (pbk.)
 1. Goldfish--Juvenile literature. [1. Goldfish. 2. Pets.] I. Title.
II. Series.
 SF458.G6G36 2003
 639.3'7484--dc21
                  2002151595

**Acknowledgments**
The author and publishers are grateful to the following for permission to reproduce copyright material:
Alamy pp. **5** (© Eureka), **26** (© Sami Sarkis Images); © Capstone Global Library Ltd. pp. **27** (Aylesbury Studios), **8**, **12**, **14**, **15**, **16**, **17**, **19**, **22**, **24**, **25** (Haddon Davies), **10**, **11**, **13**, **18** (Tudor Photography); Corbis pp. **9** (© Michael Keller), **20** (© DK Limited), **21** (© Michael Boys); Dave Bevan p. **23**; Dorling Kindersley pp. **6**, **7** (Neil Fletcher); Photolibrary p. **4** (Juniors Bildarchiv).

Cover photograph of goldfish reproduced with permission of Photolibrary (Juniors Bildarchiv).

The publishers would like to thank Judy Tuma for her invaluable assistance in the preparation of this book.

Every effort has been made to contact copyright holders of any material reproduced in this book. Any omissions will be rectified in subsequent printings if notice is given to the publisher.

This picture shows the different parts of a goldfish's body. You can see what each part is used for.

Tail for pushing and steering.

Smooth body for swimming.

Scaly skin for protection.

Eyes for seeing.

**Fins** for steering, braking, and balancing.

**Gills** for taking in **oxygen** from the water.

Mouth for gulping in water and food.

# Goldfish Babies

Goldfish **hatch** from eggs. The female lays thousands of eggs in the water. The eggs are sticky and look like blobs of jelly.

Goldfish eggs are the size of pinheads. They stick to plants.

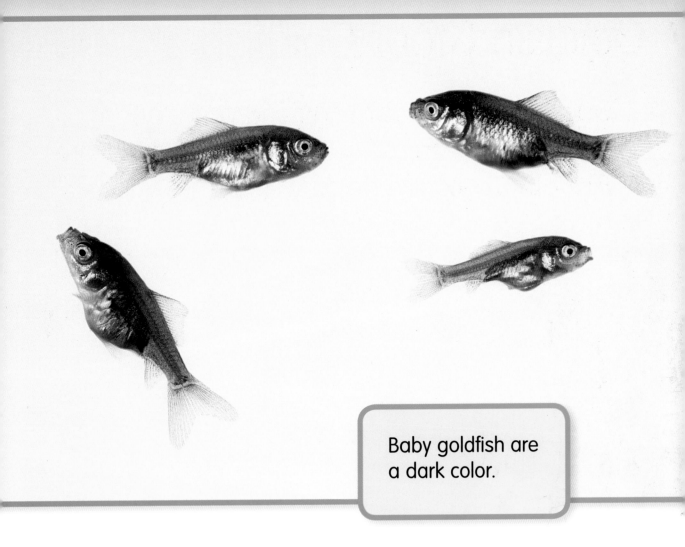

Baby goldfish are a dark color.

The baby goldfish are called fry. When they are about four months old, they begin to get their shiny adult color.

# Choosing Your Goldfish

You should buy your goldfish from a good pet store. Goldfish that you get from other places may not be healthy.

Watch the fish swimming to check that they are healthy.

Choose fish with bright, clear eyes and shiny skin. They should not swim slowly, or have split or damaged **fins** or tails.

A healthy fish should be active, with upright fins.

# Setting Up the Tank

Your fish need a tank to live in. A tank that holds two gallons of water will have room for two small fish.

Place your tank away from bright sunlight.

First, put **gravel** from the pet store in the bottom of your tank. Then fill the tank with water from the sink. Ask an adult to help you fix a water **filter** to the tank. It will help keep the water clean.

water filter

Fill the tank with water up to two inches from the tank top. You need to fill the tank with water 24 hours before you bring your fish home.

# Putting in Plants

It is a good idea to put some water plants into your tank. You can dig small holes in the **gravel** and push in the plants.

There are lots of different types of water plants. Ask your pet store to help you choose the best plants for your tank.

Plants are useful because they make **oxygen** for your fish to breathe. Your fish will also like to swim and hide among their leaves.

You can cover your tank with a hood that has a light.

# Welcome Home

You can carry your fish home in a plastic bag of water. Keep your fish in the bag and float it in your tank for 20 minutes.

Do not tip your fish into the tank right away. the different water **temperatures** may shock your goldfish and make them sick.

This makes sure that the temperature of the water in the bag is the same as in the tank. Then let your fish swim out of the bag into the tank.

When you need to move your fish, do not touch them with your hands. Use a net or jar.

# Feeding Time

You can buy special goldfish food from a pet store. Occasionally you can give your fish little pieces of boiled potato, or boiled, chopped spinach leaves.

Special fish flakes give your fish the goodness they need.

Always remove any leftover food, to stop the water getting dirty.

Feed your fish every morning and evening.
Take care not to give your fish too much food.
Too much food will make the water dirty.

# Cleaning the Tank

It is important to take care of the tank to keep your fish healthy. Your goldfish will quickly become sick in a dirty tank. Every day, check that the water is clean. Every two weeks, clean the entire tank.

Clean any green **algae** off the inside of the glass with a special sponge.

Take out only half of the old water. Put this water into a bucket and place your goldfish in the bucket. Clean the tank and gravel thoroughly. Fill up the tank with clean water and put the goldfish back in.

You can use a **siphon tube** to take some water out of your tank.

# Growing Up

Goldfish get bigger as they become adults. Watch how big your fish grow and make sure that your tank does not get crowded.

Fish that are about three inches long are the best size for your tank.

Some parks and zoos have ponds with goldfish in them!

If your goldfish grow longer than five inches, they should be moved into a larger tank or a backyard pond. Never put your goldfish into lakes, rivers, or streams.

# Healthy Goldfish

Goldfish will stay healthy if you care for them properly. Check your goldfish every day. If you think your goldfish look sick, call your **veterinarian**.

The veterinarian will be able to tell you what is wrong with your goldfish.

If a fish is sick, it is best to move it into a different tank until it is better.

If a fish seems to be moving slowly, it may not be healthy. Drooping **fins** or white spots on its skin are also signs of sickness.

# Your Pet Goldfish

Goldfish make great pets and are fun to keep. But you must be a good pet owner and care for them properly.

Your goldfish will depend on you for all their needs.

If you go on vacation, make sure that someone looks after your goldfish. Ask a friend or neighbor to come over every day.

Always make sure that your goldfish have the right food and that the tank is clean.

# Old Age

If you look after your goldfish well, they can live for many years. They do not need any special care as they get older.

A common goldfish can live for up to 25 years!

Caring for your fish will help you learn how to treat animals properly.

Older goldfish should be cared for just like younger fish. It is still important to keep their tank clean and to feed them every day.

# Useful Tips

- Wash your hands before and after you clean out the tank or feed your fish.

- Never tap the glass of the tank. This will anger or scare your fish.

- Always keep the tank out of reach of cats and other pets. It may be a good idea to fit a special cover to your goldfish tank.

- Let your goldfish get used to the tank for two weeks before you add any more fish.

- When you are cleaning the tank, put your fish in a clean container with some of the water from the tank.

- Never keep your fish in a goldfish bowl. There will not be enough **oxygen** for them to breathe.

# Fact File

- Goldfish were first kept as pets by Chinese people thousands of years ago.

- The oldest goldfish on record was thought to be over 49 years old when it died.

- Some common goldfish can grow to be 15 inches long.

- Not all goldfish are a gold color. They can be yellow, red, bronze, white, blue, black, and a mixture of these colors.

- A female goldfish lays 1,000 to 3,000 eggs at a time.

- Many kinds of goldfish have been raised to have special features, such as long **fins** or upturned eyes.

# Glossary

**algae**  tiny plantlike organisms that form a thin, green film on the walls of the tank

**filter**  machine attached to the side of the fish tank that keeps the water clean

**fins**  flaps of skin that grow on a fish's body

**gills**  part of a fish's body that takes oxygen from the water so the fish can breathe

**gravel**  tiny rocks

**hatch**  when baby fish come out of their eggs

**oxygen**  gas that animals need to breathe to stay alive

**siphon tube**  piece of tube that can suck water upwards

**temperature**  how hot or cold something is

**veterinarian**  specially trained animal doctor

# More Books to Read

An older reader can help you with these books.

Barnes, Julia. *Pet Pals: Pet Goldfish*. Strongsville, OH: Gareth Stevens Publishing, 2006.

Blizin Gillis, Jennifer. *Read and Learn: Goldfish*. Chicago, IL: Heinemann Library, 2004.

Boyer Binns, Tristan. *Keeping Pets: Freshwater Fish*. Chicago, IL: Heinemann Library, 2006.

Doering Tourville, Amanda. *Flutter and Float: Bringing Home Goldfish*. Mankato, MN: Picture Window Books, 2008.

Macaulay, Kelley. *Pet Care: Goldfish*. New York: Crabtree Publishing Company, 2004.

# Index